Mardi Gras

Dianne M. MacMillan

Reading Consultant:

Michael P. French, Ph.D.
Bowling Green State University

—Best Holiday Books—

Enslow Publishers, Inc.

44 Fadem Road	PO Box 38
Box 699	Aldershot
Springfield, NJ 07081	Hants GU12 6BP
USA	UK

To my husband, Jim, who shared
Mardi Gras with me.

Acknowledgments
The author wishes to thank Terrence Fitzmorris, professor
of Louisiana history at Tulane University, for his
careful review of the manuscript.

Library of Congress Cataloging-in-Publication Data

MacMillan, Dianne.
    Mardi Gras / Dianne M. MacMillan; reading consultant, Michael P. French.
      p. cm. — (Best holiday books.)
    Includes index.
    Summary: Explains the history and customs of Mardi Gras, the significance of the holiday,
the many ways in which it is celebrated, and how the celebrations vary according to location.
    ISBN 0-89490-819-7
    1. Carnival—Juvenile literature. 2. Carnival—United States—Juvenile literature.
[1. Mardi Gras.] I. Title. II. Series.
GT4180.M33 1997
394.2'5—dc20
                                        96-43563
                                           CIP
                                         AC

Printed in the United States of America

10 9 8 7 6 5 4 3 2 1

Illustration Credits: © Camirand, pp. 34, 36; © Diane C. Lyell, pp. 21, 28, 30, 37;
Dianne M. MacMillan, pp. 6, 24, 29, 40, 41; James R. MacMillan, pp. 4, 8, 11, 14, 16,
18, 19, 20, 31.

Cover Illustration: Oscar C. Williams

Contents

"Throw me something! Throw me something!"

A Special Tuesday

"Throw me something! Throw me something! Mister, throw me something!" Thousands of people with outstretched arms shout to the passing floats. The beautiful floats decorated with gold leaf paper roll slowly down the street. People ride on the floats. They wear colorful costumes and masks. Plastic bead necklaces and pretend gold coins whirl through the air. The masked float riders, called "maskers," toss the beads to the crowd. Women, men, and children reach to grab the beads. Singing, shouting, and music are everywhere.

Many in the crowd are dressed up as Gypsies,

This mother and daughter are dancers who entertain the carnival crowd.

gorillas, showgirls, skeletons, and cowboys. Men with clarinets and trumpets play Dixieland music. Some people dance behind the musicians. Everyone is celebrating a special Tuesday holiday. It began hundreds of years ago in France. It is like New Year's Eve and Halloween all mixed together. This is Mardi Gras (MAR-dee GRA).

Each year in some cities across the United States people celebrate Mardi Gras. In the southern United States along the Gulf Coast, Mardi Gras can be traced back to 1703. The French first settled in this part of our country. They brought the Mardi Gras holiday with them. In cities like Mobile, Alabama; Galveston, Texas; and New Orleans, Louisiana, Mardi Gras is a two-hundred-year-old tradition.

Let's find out more about this joyful celebration.

In France people long ago paraded a fat ox down the street on Mardi Gras.

How Mardi Gras Began

Long ago there were many celebrations that welcomed spring. People celebrated in hopes that their animals and crops would be plentiful in the coming season. Mardi Gras was part of the spring festival in France. Mardi Gras means "Fat Tuesday." During the celebration, the people paraded a fat ox down the street.

For hundreds of years, Mardi Gras has been celebrated on the Tuesday before Ash Wednesday. Ash Wednesday is the first day of Lent. Lent is the six weeks of time before the Christian holiday of Easter. For many years, Christians did not eat meat, cheese, eggs, or butter during Lent. They fasted, which means they ate no food or only small amounts. Knowing that they would soon be fasting, the days before Lent became a time of feasting and partying.

In England, the day before Lent was called Pancake Tuesday. People made stacks and stacks of pancakes. They stopped cooking when all of the eggs and butter and milk were gone. In Germany, the day was called Fastnacht (Eve of Fast). The people baked a special rectangular doughnut. The doughnuts were filled with molasses. Then the doughnuts were dunked in tea.

The French and Spanish called the days before Lent "carnival." The word comes from the Latin words *carne* and *vale*, which means "farewell meat." Carnival season begins on January 6, or Twelfth Night. It is the twelfth night after Christmas. Christians believe that the Wise Men or Three Kings brought gifts to the baby Jesus on this day.

Carnival is filled with parties and parades.

Each week there are more and more activities until finally the season ends with the joyous, merry-making day of Mardi Gras. Every year the date of Mardi Gras is different. It can fall on any Tuesday from February 3 to March 9. But it is always forty-six days before Easter.

In 1699, French explorers landed at the mouth of the Mississippi River. The date was March 3.

More and more people gather as the time grows closer to the parade start.

They set up camp on the river's west bank. Back in France, their country was celebrating Mardi Gras. The leader named their camp Pointe du Mardi Gras (Point of Mardi Gras). Three years later, the French founded a settlement near present day Mobile, Alabama. The first Mardi Gras celebration took place in Mobile. The people held a party, or ball. They wore costumes and masks. Everyone danced just as they had done in France.

In 1718, the French founded the town of Nouvelle Orleans (New Orleans) in what is now Louisiana. French settlers loved the Mardi Gras celebration. They looked forward to the grand masked balls each year. From the early beginnings in Mobile and New Orleans, Mardi Gras has grown and changed.

Secret Clubs and Parades

In 1857, six young men in New Orleans formed a special carnival club. They called their club the "Mistick Krewe of Comus." Comus was a Roman god of partying in mythology. The men paraded on Mardi Gras night with two floats. They wore costumes and masks. African-American servants carried torches and walked alongside the floats. The people of New Orleans were delighted.

The club became known as Comus. The members invented the word "krewe" to stand for their secret club. They also began the tradition of calling a krewe after a name from mythology.

Each krewe parades sometime during Carnival or on the day of Mardi Gras.

Having a parade with floats became a new part of the holiday.

Other people wanted to form secret krewes. Soon there were krewes called Twelfth Night Revelers, Rex, Momus, and Proteus. In the beginning, the krewe members were only men. Later women formed their own krewes. Some krewes have both men and women members. The

Krewe of Little Rascals in New Orleans is made up of boys and girls ages five to sixteen. Today there are more than one hundred krewes in New Orleans. Some members belong to more than one krewe.

Many other cities have krewes. People in Mobile call their secret clubs "mystic societies." There are over fifty mystic societies. New ones are formed every year.

Many times the identity of the members is kept secret. Sometimes membership in a krewe is passed down from father to son. The krewe members spend the year planning the parties and parades for next year's Mardi Gras celebration.

During the carnival season, each krewe gives a fancy ball. There is music and dancing. Men dress in tuxedos, and women wear long evening gowns. The guests wear elaborate masks. In some cities, the guests wear costumes to the ball. Often a king and queen are chosen at the ball. They will "reign" over the parade and ride in a special float.

Many krewes entertain their guests at the ball

Krewes spend the year planning for next year's parade and Mardi Gras celebration. This float is shaped like a paddle wheel riverboat. A Dixieland band is playing music.

by putting on plays. These plays, called tableaus, show scenes from history or legends. The themes of the tableaus are kept secret until the ball. Guests look foward to watching these plays.

Many of the balls are private. Only krewe members and their guests are invited. But the parades are for everyone. During carnival season, each krewe parades on different streets on an assigned day. Some krewes parade in the daytime, others at night. Sometimes there are as many as seventy parades within a few weeks. Schedules of parades are printed in the newspapers and local magazines.

Every parade has a theme chosen by the krewe. Each float carries out the theme. Like the plays at the ball, the themes are about events in history or famous legends and stories. Most of the floats are pulled by trailers. Long ago the floats were built on top of wooden wagons. Horses pulled the wagons through the streets. People carrying torches walked alongside to light up the float. Today many floats are covered with neon lights. Others have moving parts.

Floats in the night parades are covered with lights. There have been Mardi Gras parades since 1857.

Some huge floats are as tall as two-story buildings.

The float that carries the king and queen is always special. The most famous king is Rex. He waves to the crowds from his bandwagon. His attendants are dressed in purple, green, and gold. These are the colors of Mardi Gras.

Some krewes, such as Bacchus, choose a famous person like a movie or television star to be their parade's king. Dukes and maids dressed in costumes ride in another float behind the king's float.

A parade might have twenty or more floats. There are also lots of marching bands. Larger parades may have as many as sixty different bands marching with them. The Rex parade, one

Each krewe chooses a king. This krewe's king looks down on his subjects watching from below.

This shop is selling Mardi Gras doubloons.

of the largest in New Orleans, may have over three thousand people riding in floats and marching. Parades last from two to four hours. All of the parades are free to watch.

Krewe members pay for the cost of building the floats and for their costumes. They also spend thousands of dollars on souvenirs. Souvenirs are things that people keep to remind

It is fun to collect Mardi Gras souvenirs.

them of special events. Mardi Gras souvenirs are called "throws" because the people riding the floats, called "maskers," throw them to the crowds. Popular throws are plastic bead necklaces, plastic cups, and aluminum coins. The coins are stamped with the krewe's symbol on one side. The other side has the parade's theme.

These special coins are called doubloons. They are named for Spanish gold pieces used in the 1500s. The first doubloon was thrown by Rex in 1960. Since then krewes have stamped special coins each year to throw. Whether they are beads or coins, throws make Mardi Gras parades different from all other parades.

Every year it costs a lot of money to buy all the throws. In recent years, some krewes have stopped parading. Their members could no longer afford to pay for the floats and throws. But new krewes have started up and continue the tradition.

Carnival

The carnival season begins on Twelfth Night, or January 6. Each year one of the krewes in New Orleans, called the Phunny Phorty Phellows, rides in a streetcar on January 6. A sign on the side announces, "It's Carnival Time."

In the evening, many people attend large balls. They wear fancy clothes with masks or costumes.

Everyone loves going to carnival parties. A popular tradition is eating King Cakes. King Cakes look like large oval doughnuts. They are decorated with purple, green, and gold icing. Most of the cakes contain a small doll. The doll

A singer entertains the crowd with his impersonation of Elvis Presley.

symbolizes the baby Jesus who was visited by the Three Wise Men on January 6. Whoever finds the small doll has to help host the next party or buy the next cake.

Some cakes have a small golden bean in them instead of a doll. King Cake parties are very popular. More than half a million King Cakes are eaten every year in New Orleans. In Biloxi, Mississippi, bakers start baking King Cakes as soon as Christmas is over. They want to be sure that they will have enough made when Carnival begins.

As the time draws closer to Mardi Gras, there are more events. Cities have art exhibits, concerts, beauty pageants, stage shows, and costume contests. Galveston, Texas, has an annual rugby tournament, a game similar to soccer and football. And of course, every week brings more masked balls and parades. Excitement builds and builds.

Other Mardi Gras Celebrations

Every year more cities across the country are joining in the fun of Mardi Gras. Mobile, Alabama's celebration, the oldest in our country, is similar to New Orleans' celebration. However, instead of each secret club selecting a king and queen, there is only one king and queen for the whole celebration. The royal couple is chosen at a special ball the Saturday before Mardi Gras. It is a great honor to be selected.

Mobile has another tradition that is different. Along with the plastic beads and trinkets, maskers throw moon pies at the crowd. Moon pies are round and are four inches wide. The pies look like cakes. They are filled with cream and chocolate icing. Each pie is covered with clear plastic. The pies are named after the company that first made them.

At one time, maskers threw boxes of Cracker Jack. The parade organizers were afraid someone might be hurt. Cracker Jack was banned as a throw. The maskers wanted to throw some other kind of food. They discovered moon pies. It is believed that the first moon pie was thrown in the Comic Cowboys' parade in 1953.

People along the parade route try to catch the pies as they are tossed from the floats. Some societies have special moon pies in different flavors. Some pies are banana or cherry flavored. The special pies are wrapped in silver paper. The club emblem is stamped on the wrapper. It is estimated that 250,000 pies are thrown each day the last two weeks of carnival. The maskers also throw pieces of hard candy and bags of popcorn or peanuts.

Galveston, Texas, has many events during the carnival season. There are parades, beauty pageants, art exhibits, and balls. On the Sunday before Mardi Gras, the annual Munchkin Parade takes place. Children ages four to fourteen dress in costumes and ride on decorated floats. After the parade, the Galveston Symphony presents a children's concert.

On the day of Mardi Gras, Galveston carries on the traditions of Pancake Tuesday started in England. There are pancake races, a

Pom pom girls are throwing beads from their float.

pancake cook-off, and pancake-eating and pancake-flipping contests. The women of Galveston compete against women from the country of Australia.

In San Luis Obispo, California, the largest Mardi Gras celebration west of the Mississippi River takes place. Each year downtown streets are closed off. In the afternoon, families in costumes line the sidewalks. Carnival booths sell

Face painting is popular on Mardi Gras.

food and have games. Children have their faces painted.

Many events copy things done in New Orleans. There are gumbo cookoffs or contests. Gumbo is a meat or seafood stew made with vegetables. It is popular in New Orleans. People taste each gumbo entry and choose the one they like best.

Musicians play Dixieland music. Other

These Cub Scouts are riding on a float in the parade.

This Dixieland band is playing music on a street corner.

entertainers sing and dance for the audience. Finally it is time for the parade. Krewes and area businessmen have built the floats. Forty to fifty floats roll down the street. Children and adults crowd close hoping to catch some beads. After the parade, there is a costume ball and dinner.

In other places, neighborhoods, and small communities, people put on their own Mardi Gras parades. Families work together to build the floats. Children dress in costumes. Boy Scouts and Girl Scouts march in the parade. High school bands play music. Everyone has a great time.

Mardi Gras in Canada

Many cities in Canada celebrate carnival season and Mardi Gras. French explorers settled in parts of Canada and brought Mardi Gras with them. Several cities combine Mardi Gras celebrations with winter sports games. Edmonton, Alberta, has a Muk-Luk Mardi Gras. This is the city's winter sports carnival.

The most famous Carnival and Mardi Gras is held in Quebec City. Quebec held its first celebration in 1864. The people welcomed the celebration. They loved having a break from the long harsh winter.

Every year since 1955, Quebec has held their

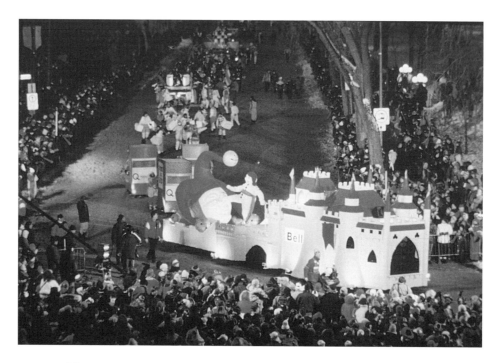

Thousands of people bundle up to watch Quebec's Mardi Gras parade.

"Carnaval de Quebec" (Carnival of Quebec). It lasts for seventeen days. It is the world's third-largest carnival after Rio de Janeiro in South America and New Orleans. Just like the carnival season in the United States, there are lots of King Cake parties, balls, and parades. But there are also many winter activities that take place outside. There are snow sculpture contests, ice canoe races across the St. Lawrence River, and Roll in the Snow events.

In 1994, over one million people took part in Quebec's carnival. The symbol of Quebec's carnival is Bonhomme, a snowman. In the beginning of January, Bonhomme arrives. The mayor of the city welcomes Bonhomme. He gives Bonhomme the "key" to the city. This is a symbol that Bonhomme is in charge of the city during carnival. A young woman is chosen to be carnival queen.

Each year an ice palace is built for Bonhomme. The palace is made from snow. It takes over nine thousand tons of ice and snow to make the palace. Fifteen men work every day for two months. When it is finished, the ice palace is seventy-five feet tall. It becomes the main attraction of carnival. Tourists love to visit the palace and take pictures of it.

People wear costumes to the annual Mardi Gras Ball. The highlight of the season is the Mardi Gras parade. The brightly lit parade has beautiful floats, clowns, and bands. More than

Bonhomme is Quebec's symbol of the city's winter carnival.

A clown is riding in the parade.

half a million people bundle up in warm clothes to watch. As carnival and Mardi Gras end, Bonhomme returns the key to the city. He bids farewell until next year's celebration.

Mardi Gras Fun

Mardi Gras is not meant to be serious. The purpose of the holiday is to have fun. People love wearing costumes and acting silly.

Instead of white horses, mules lead the king's float in the Sparta parade in New Orleans. Comus holds a goblet instead of a royal scepter. The theme song of New Orleans' Mardi Gras is a silly song called "If Ever I Cease to Love." The first verse says,

> *If ever I cease to love,*
> *If ever I cease to love,*
> *May oysters have legs,*
> *And cows lay eggs,*
> *If ever I cease to love.*

Mardi Gras Arrives

After weeks of balls and parades, Mardi Gras is here. On Tuesday morning in New Orleans, people are up early. Many dress in costumes. Some have worked on their costumes for many months, sewing on feathers and sequins. Everyone enjoys playing make-believe. Soon the sidewalks are lined with costumed people waiting for the parades.

Parades start as early as 8:00 A.M. There may be as many as five or more throughout the day. Thousands of tourists come from all over the world to take part in the day's merrymaking. Some people bring stepladders to stand on so they can get a better view of the floats. Others

A mother and her daughters are wearing *Cat in the Hat* hats for Mardi Gras.

spread out blankets and eat picnic lunches while they wait. Street vendors push carts and sell funny items like blinking bow ties, fake noses, and glowing necklaces. Others sell popcorn and cotton candy. Musicians appear to be everywhere, playing and marching through the crowd.

Everyone wants souvenir throws from the

Hours before the parade begins, people line the sidewalks to get the best view.

floats. Bead necklaces are the most common. But the maskers also throw frisbees and other small plastic toys. A few lucky people will catch a gold-colored doubloon stamped with the carnival symbol.

While waiting for a parade, the crowds hope to see the Mardi Gras Indians. "Tribes" of Mardi Gras Indians have marched for more than one hundred years. No one knows how they began but members are African Creoles (people of mixed African, Native American, French, and Spanish descent).

The Mardi Gras Indians march through neighborhoods dancing to music. They do not have a set parade route and can appear anywhere. Mardi Gras Indians wear beautiful costumes covered with thousands of beads, sequins, rhinestones, and feathers. All of the designs of flowers or animals are sewn by hand. Some of the costumes take months to make. They are worn only once. As the Mardi Gras Indians pass by, many people join in behind dancing to the rhythm of their tunes.

Another favorite parade is put on by the Zulu

krewe. Zulu is the oldest African-American krewe. They have been marching since 1909. The Zulu parade is held early in the morning. Many of their maskers wear grass skirts. A lucky person in the crowd might catch a valuable throw—a decorated coconut, symbol of the Zulus. The streets and sidewalks overflow with people laughing, singing, and dancing. In the evening after the last parade, the final costume balls are held. At midnight, police blow horns. The horns let people know it is time to go home. Mardi Gras is over. Street sweepers begin cleaning up tons of confetti, plastic cups, and beads.

This year's Mardi Gras is a memory. But in a few days, the krewes are busy planning next year's themes and floats. Everyone looks forward to the season of the year when people of all races and backgrounds come together for the magic that is Mardi Gras.

Glossary

Ash Wednesday—The first day of Lent, the six-week period before Easter.

ball—A fancy party.

carnival—The days from January 6 until Mardi Gras that are filled with parties and parades.

doubloon—A Spanish gold coin used a long time ago.

fast—To not eat food or to eat only small amounts of food.

King Cakes—Special cakes baked during carnival season. They contain a small doll or bean. Whoever finds the doll must give the next party.

krewe—The name for secret clubs that plan Mardi Gras parades and balls.

Lent—A time of preparing for Easter.

maskers—Costumed float riders.

souvenirs—Something kept as a reminder of a person, place, or event.

tableau—A play performed at a ball by krewe members.

theme—The main idea or subject of something.

tradition—To do the same thing in the same way every year.

throws—Souvenirs tossed to the crowds from the Mardi Gras floats.

Index